# ANIMAL
## WORLDS OF WONDER

## STERLING CHILDREN'S BOOKS
### New York

An Imprint of Sterling Publishing Co., Inc.
1166 Avenue of the Americas
New York, NY 10036

First published in the UK in 2018 by 20 Watt,
an imprint of Bonnier Books UK,
The Plaza, 535 King's Road, London, SW10 0SZ
www.bonnierbooks.co.uk

ISBN 978-1-4549-3550-6

Distributed in Canada by Sterling Publishing Co., Inc.
c/o Canadian Manda Group, 664 Annette Street
Toronto, Ontario, M6S 2C8, Canada

For information about custom editions, special sales, and premium and corporate purchases, please contact Sterling Special Sales at 800-805-5489 or specialsales@sterlingpublishing.com.

Manufactured in China

Lot #:
2 4 6 8 10 9 7 5 3 1
06/19

sterlingpublishing.com

# ANIMAL
# WORLDS OF WONDER

WRITTEN BY ANITA GANERI

ILLUSTRATED BY MADDY VIAN

STERLING CHILDREN'S BOOKS
New York

# CONTENTS

# WORLDS OF WONDER

From the deepest depths of the sea to the peaks of the highest mountains, Earth has an amazing variety of places where animals and plants can live.

There are bone-dry deserts, rolling grasslands, rushing rivers, icy poles, fabulous forests—the list goes on and on. The place where an animal lives, and that provides it with the food, water, and shelter it needs to survive, is called a habitat. Some habitats are enormous—the sea covers two-thirds of Earth. Others are tiny, such as a single leaf on a tree, or the underside of a garden stone.

Climate (the weather that a place has over a long time) and temperature are the most important factors in making a habitat. Habitats can be wet, dry, hot, cold, teeming with life, or barren and bare. As the climate changes, so does the habitat.

Keel-billed toucan

Locust

Giant anteater

Mountain goat

The higher up a mountain you go, the colder and windier it gets. Different types of animals and plants adapt to live at the different levels.

Likewise, the range of animals that live in a cooler part of the ocean are different to those that live on a warm coral reef.

Throughout this book, you'll visit many of these habitats and meet the animals that live in them, from polar bears on the Arctic ice, and woodpeckers on a desert cactus, to giant pandas in their forests of bamboo. You'll find out where they live, how they live, and which other animals they share their homes with. Welcome to Earth and its many worlds of wonder.

Tiger shark

Snowy owl

# HABITATS

A habitat, and the animals, plants and non-living things found in it, are called an ecosystem. A large ecosystem, such as a forest, contains many smaller ecosystems, such as tree roots or rotting tree trunks. The different living things in an ecosystem are linked to each other in different ways, forming complex webs of life.

## ADAPTING ANIMALS

To survive in their habitat, animals must adapt or become more suited to their surroundings. To do this, they have special features and ways of behaving that have evolved over a very long time. For example, deep-sea anglerfish make their own light to help them survive in the deep sea, where it is always dark. Flamingos have curved beaks for scooping food from shallow water in the lakes where they live. Foxes have adapted to find food in cities, raiding dustbins for scraps. Camels can go for weeks without water in their dry desert homes.

Red fox

Camel

Flamingo

Triplewart seadevil

# FOOD CHAINS

The animals and plants in a habitat are linked by what they eat. These links join up to make a food chain, where each link is a meal for the next in line. Some food chains are quite simple. In the Arctic, phytoplankton (sea plants) are eaten by copepods (sea animals). In turn, the copepods are eaten by fish, the fish by seals, and the seals by polar bears. Different food chains interlink to form a food web.

Polar bear

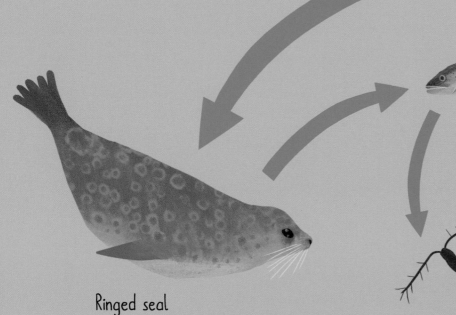

Polar cod

Phytoplankton

Copepod

Ringed seal

# HABITATS IN DANGER

All over the world, habitats are being destroyed for their resources and to make more space for humans to live and farm in. This can spell disaster for the animals living there, especially as many are not suited to surviving anywhere else. Over the last 60 years, habitat loss, together with poaching and disease, has reduced the number of western lowland gorillas in the wild by more than 60 percent.

# ANIMAL
## WORLDS OF WONDER

# ANIMALS ON LAND

Dry land provides a great variety of habitats for animals and plants to live in—mountains, grasslands, rainforests, and deserts, for starters. Each place offers many challenges for its residents to overcome.

## THE MOUNTAINS

Mountains can be cold and windy, especially as you go higher up, and more so in winter. Alpine marmots survive the plummeting winter temperatures by hibernating in burrows for up to eight months a year. Their heart and breathing rates drop, and they live off stores of fat in their bodies, laid down before the cold weather begins.

## TROPICAL RAINFOREST

Warm, humid tropical rainforests grow around the equator, where conditions are ideal for plants, and animals, to thrive. In Madagascar, leaf-tailed geckos are superbly camouflaged to avoid being seen and eaten. Leaf-cutter ants use their incredible strength to snip leaves to use in their "gardens" where they grow fungus for food.

Leaf cutter ants

# THE DESERT

Deserts are often hot and dry—hostile conditions for animals. In Australia, the water-holding frog survives very dry spells in a cool burrow underground. It stores precious water in its body, forming a cocoon of skin around itself to stop this water being lost. It can stay like this for up to five years, until the rains come.

# GRASSLAND

On the grasslands, large black beetles take advantage of other animals by recycling their dung. Using its back legs, a dung beetle rolls the dung into a ball, up to ten times its own weight. Then the beetle buries the ball in the ground to use later as food, or for laying its eggs in.

# FAST HUNTERS

A cheetah is perfectly designed for chasing its prey across the vast grassland plains. It is the speediest mammal on the planet, with a flexible backbone to allow it to sprint and leap. As it runs, its sharp claws grip the ground like the spikes on a running shoe.

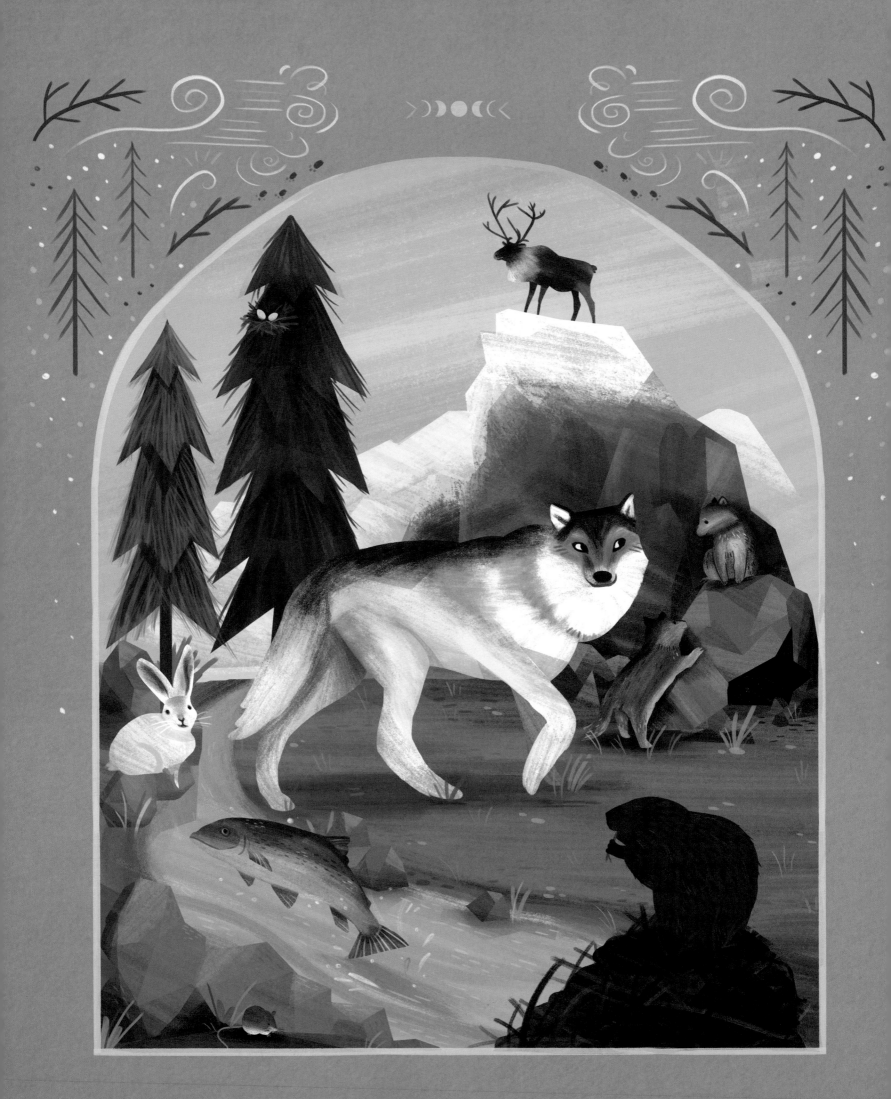

# GRAY WOLF
## CANIS LUPUS

Also known as the common wolf, or the timber wolf, the gray wolf can be found in remote areas of North America, Europe, and Asia. Because the gray wolf can adapt to eating a wide range of foods, it can survive in many different habitats, from forests to plains, mountains and Arctic tundra. This wolf lives in the wilderness of Alaska. To claim its territory, it marks certain areas with its scent and howls loudly to warn off intruders.

Gray wolves are expert predators and will eat almost anything! They mostly hunt caribou, deer, and wild boar. They will also eat smaller mammals, birds and their eggs, snakes, lizards, berries, and fish. This wolf makes the most of its Arctic environment, feasting on caribou, Alaskan hares, beavers, ground squirrels, tiny dormice, and local fish, such as chinook salmon. Wolves live and hunt in packs, working together to catch and bring down their prey. Chases can cover a lot of ground—up to 3 miles. Hunting together allows them to bring down animals that may be ten times bigger than a single wolf.

A pack may be a family group of eight to twelve wolves, with a strict hierarchy. At the top is an alpha couple, a male and female wolf that stay together for life. The rest of the pack are usually their offspring. Litters of around six cubs are born in spring, in a den, cave or hollow log. They are ready to travel with the rest of the pack at around five months old.

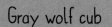

Gray wolf cub

**CARIBOU**
Hunting in packs, gray wolves can catch and kill a caribou.

**AMERICAN BEAVER**
Wolves will eat beavers, especially in the summer months.

**CHINOOK SALMON**
Sometimes, wolves will catch fish, such as the Chinook salmon, to eat.

**ALASKAN HARE**
The Alaskan hare is one of the smaller mammals that may become food for the gray wolf.

# GALÁPAGOS TORTOISE
## *CHELONOIDIS NIGRA VANDENBURGHI*

On the Galápagos Islands, off the coast of Ecuador, South America, live the world's largest tortoises. These gigantic reptiles weigh almost half a ton, and grow up to 5 feet long. They have stumpy legs with sharp claws, long, scaly necks, and huge, domed, bony shells. They are among the longest-lived animals on Earth—the oldest known individual was 152 years old. They tend to spend time in small groups, mostly eating and sleeping.

Galápagos dove

**LAND IGUANA**
Land iguanas also allow finches to pick ticks from between their scales.

This huge tortoise lives on Isabela Island, on the slopes and in the crater of the Alcedo volcano, one of six volcanoes on the island. After warming up in the sun, it spends most of the day foraging for cacti and other plants to eat. It gets the moisture it needs from dew and plants, and can go for months without anything to eat and drink.

**VERMILLION FLYCATCHER**
Vermillion flycatchers mainly eat insects, which they catch and eat mid-air.

Galápagos tortoises sometimes let certain species of finch groom them. They stick out their neck, and then the birds hop closer and feed on the ticks on their skin. This relationship suits both animals—the finch gets a meal and the tortoise stays healthy. However, sometimes tortoises will trick these birds, crushing them with their shells and then eating them.

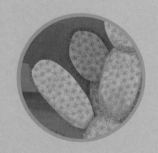

**OPUNTIA CACTUS**
Galápagos tortoises, land iguanas, and many birds of the Galápagos eat the pads and fruits of this cactus.

Recently, the Alcedo tortoise's habitat was threatened by wild goats that ate the plants it relied on for food. Today, the goats have been removed from the island, so that the plants, and the tortoises, can recover.

**MANGROVE FINCH**
Mangrove finches have special beaks for picking insects off of tree bark.

# POLAR BEAR
## *URSUS MARITIMUS*

This magnificent polar bear lives in the Arctic and is perfectly adapted to its icy home. It has a thick, white coat to keep it warm, with only the soles of its feet and the tip of its nose not covered in fur. For grip, its sharp claws dig into the ice, and bumps on the soles of its feet stop it from slipping. Polar bears are excellent swimmers; using their huge front paws as paddles, they can swim for several hours at a time over long distances.

Weighing in at more than half a ton, the polar bear is the world's largest carnivore. They hunt for seals on ice-covered coastlines, pouncing when they surface to breathe. A polar bear has such a sharp sense of smell that it can sniff out a seal half a mile away, and up to 3 feet under the ice. They will also eat seabirds, walruses, berries, and seaweed if there are no seals available.

As apex hunters, with no predators of their own, polar bears do not have much competition for food, though Arctic foxes will sometimes prey on the seals and fish that polar bears eat.

Female polar bears give birth to litters of two to three cubs inside dens, which they build inside snowdrifts. They have to have eaten enough in the prior months to survive for months without eating. Cubs weigh just one pound at birth and nurse from their mothers for almost two years before setting off into their habitats alone.

Arctic fox

### WALRUS
Walruses have a thick layer of blubber (fat) under their skin—this makes them a good meal for polar bears.

### BELUGA WHALE
Polar bears may also hunt belugas, if these white whales become trapped in the ice.

### SNOW GOOSE
Snow geese breed in the Arctic in spring, then spend the winter farther south where it is warmer.

### BEARDED SEAL
Seals, such as bearded and ringed seals, are a polar bear's favorite prey.

# KING COBRA
## OPHIOPHAGUS HANNAH

When this king cobra feels threatened, it lifts the front part of its body off the ground, and fans out the hood of skin around its neck. To look more menacing, it makes a sound like a growling dog and slithers forwards to attack. Growing to around 13 ft long, the majestic king cobra is the world's longest venomous snake. With a single bite, it can deliver enough powerful venom to kill an Indian elephant in just 15 minutes.

Luckily, king cobras are usually quite shy and like to hide away in their highland forest homes. They move through the trees, in the water and along the ground, preying on other snakes—even venomous pit vipers and rat snakes. They track their prey by smell, "tasting" the air with their forked tongues. When they get close enough, they strike, then swallow their victim whole. It can take several hours to swallow a large meal, but the cobra will not have to eat again for several weeks.

Though they are deadly hunters, king cobras have predators, too—mongooses. These mammals are the only predator to kill and eat venomous snakes, ducking and diving out the way of the cobra's deadly bite.

Female king cobras lay large clutches of up to 50 eggs in spring or early summer. They build complicated nests with two layers—at the bottom is a chamber for the eggs and on top is a chamber for the mother.

Rat snake

**BENGAL TIGER**
These hunters kill and eat gaur, deer, and buffalo, but avoid the deadly venom of king cobras.

**GAUR**
Also called Indian bison, gaur live in herds to protect themselves from predators and will fight off tigers!

**MALABAR PIT VIPER**
Malabar pit vipers are a favorite food of king cobras.

**GREAT INDIAN HORNBILL**
Groups of Indian hornbills gather in the trees, feeding on fruit, such as juicy figs.

# JAPANESE MACAQUE
## MACACA FUSCATA

Also known as snow monkeys, Japanese macaques are hardy creatures that live in the forests and mountains of Japan, where snow covers the ground for many months each year. These medium-size monkeys have thick, silky fur that allows them to stay warm in winter, even when temperatures dip below 5°F. They are the only primates that live year-round in snowy conditions. This clever macaque is using another ingenious way of escaping the cold—it is sitting in the natural hot springs where it lives. Intelligent and playful, Japanese macaques like to take advantage of the snow by having snowball fights.

These macaques live in large social groups called troops, with around 40 monkeys. There is a strict pecking order in the troop. The troop spends its day feeding, playing, and grooming. Grooming helps to strengthen the bonds between the macaques and is also important for keeping their fur clean.

Japanese woodpecker

To keep the troop together, macaques make cooing noises, and they also have special alarm calls to warn of danger. They are very clever animals, who are experts at avoiding predators like foxes and mountain hawk eagles.

In spring and summer, the monkeys eat flowers, young leaves, seeds, and fruits, while in fall and winter they eat fungi, nuts, insects, roots—and even tree bark!

**RED FOX**
Red foxes are opportunistic feeders, eating anything from berries to small fish.

**RACCOON DOG**
Raccoon dogs increase their body size by up to 50 percent before winter to prepare for hibernation.

**JAPANESE WOODPECKER**
These birds compete with macaques and other insectivores for food.

**SIKA DEER**
Sika deer eat plants and fruit knocked down from the trees by overhead macaques.

# GORILLA
## GORILLA GORILLA GORILLA

Western lowland gorillas live in the Congo rainforest, in Central Africa. They form groups, called troops, of around 30, led by an older adult male, like the one shown here. He is sometimes called a "silverback" because of the wide streak of gray across his black fur. There are also younger males, together with females and their young, which spend their time in play and swinging through the trees. The silverback organizes the troop's activities, including waking up, feeding, and going to sleep.

Because of their large size, gorillas are usually found on the ground. They are mainly vegetarian, feeding on a diet of fruit, roots, shoots, and tree bark. In a single day, they will roam between 0.5 and 2.5 miles to pick fruit to eat. Gorillas must compete with the many plant-eating animals and birds in the rainforest, including gray parrots, giant forest hogs, and sitatundas, for the fruit and plants available, while insectivores, such as guerezas, help stop insects from chomping away at the gorillas' food.

Gorillas are most active in the morning, when they feed for a few hours. At midday, they take a nap in a nest made from leaves and branches, then feed again in the afternoon. At night, they build another nest for sleeping in.

Gray parrot

Today, these amazing animals are under serious threat. Their forest home is being destroyed to make space for farming and homes, and they are being hunted for their meat.

### GUEREZA COLOBUS
This acrobatic monkey leaps from tree to tree, on the lookout for leaves and fruit.

### SITATUNGA
The sitatunga is an antelope that lives in swamps in the forest and feeds on swamp plants.

### AFRICAN FOREST ELEPHANT
These elephants can detect rumbles from other herds up to 10 miles away.

### GIANT FOREST HOG
Giant forest hogs are large wild pigs, with bristly manes and short, sharp, curved tusks.

A jaguar can catch a caiman twice its size in its powerful jaws

# JAGUAR
## PANTHERA ONCA

Today, jaguars are found in Central and South America, mainly in the Amazon rainforest. In the past they had a much larger area to roam, and lived as far north as Arizona, North America. They like to live near rivers and swamps, and are excellent swimmers and climbers. Unless it is breeding time, jaguars live and hunt alone, marking out their own patch of forest. They can be highly aggressive in protecting their territory.

Like most other big cats, the jaguar has a muscular body, large head, and powerful jaws. It is built for hunting. The top predators in the rainforest, jaguars usually come out at dawn and dusk to find food. Their golden-brown fur is dappled with large dark spots, and this patterning gives them great camouflage so they can hide among the shadows.

Red-bellied piranha

A jaguar's favorite prey includes wild pigs, tapir, and capybaras, but they will also catch caiman crocodiles, turtles, sloths, and fish, including the carnivorous red-bellied piranha. Its teeth are sharp and strong enough to bite through an animal's skull in a single bite.

Thousands of jaguars were once killed for their beautiful coats. Today, they are protected by law but still face danger. Their rainforest home is being destroyed, which means that there is less and less prey for the jaguars to hunt.

**SCARLET MACAW**
Macaws fly all over the rainforest in search of fruits and berries to eat.

**CAPYBARA**
These gentle, social animals sometimes look after the babies of other animals.

**KEEL-BILLED TOUCAN**
These playful birds will play with their food, throwing and catching fruit in the air.

# RED KANGAROO
## MACROPUS RUFUS

Using its enormously strong back legs, a red kangaroo hops along the ground, covering an astonishing 30 feet in a single bound. It travels long distances every day to find enough food, and hopping saves huge amounts of energy, compared to walking or running.

This red kangaroo lives in hot, dry grasslands in Australia, in a group of up to 10 animals, called a mob. It spends the morning grazing on grasses and shrubs, then rests in the shade during the hottest part of the day. To cool down, it may lick its forearms until the fur is soaking wet — as the saliva evaporates, it cools their body temperature. They begin grazing again in the cooler evening.

Male red kangaroos are the largest marsupials, standing up to 6.5 feet tall. Females are smaller, and have darker fur. The males will sometimes fight each other over potential mates, throwing powerful punches as they box each other with their strong back legs.

The kangaroo doesn't have many predators, but dingoes and wild dogs will hunt them if they cross paths. Eagles will also sometimes hunt smaller kangaroos when food is scarce, and will feed on kangaroo carrion (dead bodies).

Kangaroos survive on very little water and can go for months without drinking at all.

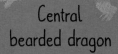

Central bearded dragon

Thorny devil

29

**WEDGE-TAILED EAGLE**
This eagle is the largest bird of prey in all of Australia.

**DROMEDARIES**
Dromedaries, sometimes called feral camels, were introduced to Australia during the 19th century.

**DINGO**
Dingoes will form large hunting packs to attack larger prey.

**EUROPEAN WILD RABBIT**
These rabbits have impacted the vegetation available in Australia, leaving less food for other grazing animals.

# GIANT PANDA
## AILUROPODA MELANOLEUCA

With its striking black-and-white fur coat, the giant panda is one of the most recognizable creatures on Earth. These stockily-built bears live in the thick bamboo forests that grow high up in the mountains of south-west China. Their habitat is cold and damp, but their fur is thick and waterproof to keep them warm and dry.

Pandas sometimes eat eggs and small animals, but most of their diet is made up of bamboo. They have specially adapted wrist bones for gripping the bamboo, and powerful jaws and large back teeth for crushing the tough stems. To get enough nourishment from this diet, however, pandas need to feed for around 16 hours a day, and munch around 66 lbs of bamboo. This is because, like other bears, their stomachs evolved for them to be carnivores (meat eaters).

Few animals will hunt fully grown pandas, but panda cubs are at risk from attack from Asian black bears, yellow throated martens, and some eagles.

Unlike some other bears, giant pandas don't hibernate. Instead, they travel to find better sources of bamboo or avoid extremely cold weather.

Today, giant pandas are very rare, with fewer than 2,500 left in the wild. One reason is that such a specialized diet makes them very sensitive to any changes in their habitat. If the bamboo dies or is cleared to make space for growing crops, the pandas face starvation.

Yellow-throated marten

### GOLDEN SNUB-NOSED MONKEY
Golden snub-nosed monkeys live high up in the trees, feeding on lichen and bark.

### GOLDEN TAKIN
Golden takin eat almost any vegetation within their reach, including tough oak bark and bamboo leaves.

### ASIAN BLACK BEAR
Asian black bears mostly eat plants, but will also catch giant panda cubs.

### GOLDEN PHEASANT
The brightly colored male golden pheasant can be difficult to spot because of the dense forest.

# AFRICAN ELEPHANT
## LOXODONTA AFRICANA

African elephants are the world's largest land mammals, with the males reaching a whopping 6 tons in weight. They roam the grasslands of eastern, southern, and western Africa, alongside other amazing animals, such as giraffes, lions, and gazelles.

Elephants are adapted for feeding on the grasses and trees that grow in their habitat. They use their long, flexible trunks to pluck grasses and leaves, and their tusks to strip tree bark and dig up roots which they grind up with their large teeth. To fuel its huge body, an elephant needs an enormous amount of food—around 350 pounds a day. It also needs plenty to drink and will dig holes in dried river beds to reach water.

This elephant has two oxpeckers on its back—these birds land on the elephant and pick off little parasites. They also make loud calls if they spot a potential predator in the distance, warning the elephant of danger. Other animals in the area will also listen for these calls.

African elephants live in close-knit families made up of around 10 females and their calves. Each family is led by an older female, or matriarch. Several families may join together to form a larger herd. Males leave the group and live alone. The females help to babysit each other's calves and will form a circle around them if danger threatens. Their size and strength makes the herd difficult to hunt.

Masai giraffe

### GREY CROWNED CRANE
Cranes follow giraffes and antelope around, hoping to eat bugs uncovered by these larger animals.

### HELMETED GUINEAFOWL
These birds will sometimes scavenge for food in elephant dung.

### THOMSON'S GAZELLE
Thomson's gazelles are sociable animals, often migrating with other species such as wildebeest.

### LIONESS
Lions rarely manage to hunt full grown elephants but sometimes successfully hunt their young.

# ANIMALS IN THE WATER

Water covers 71 percent of the earth's surface, and 96.5 percent of all of the world's water is found in Earth's oceans. Animals that live in lakes, rivers, and the sea have an amazing range of features and ways of behaving to help them survive in their watery habitats.

## PARROT FISH

Parrot fish use their beak-like mouths to bite chunks of coral from a reef, then grind them up to get to the tiny plants inside. Any undigested coral is excreted as sand. At night, a parrot fish wraps itself in a mucus sleeping bag which may help to hide its smell, so that it is harder for predators, such as moray eels, to find.

## LEOPARD SEAL

Leopard seals live in the icy waters of the Southern Ocean around Antarctica. They are fierce hunters, with sharp teeth and strong, streamlined bodies for swimming after their prey. They eat fish, squid, penguins, and even other seals. A thick layer of blubber (fat) under their skin helps to keep them warm in the cold water.

34

# JAPANESE SALAMANDER

One of the largest amphibians in the world, Japanese salamanders can grow up to almost 5 feet long. They live in rocky, fast-flowing streams in Japan, where their mottled brown-and-black skin helps to camouflage them against the stream bed. It breathes through its skin, which is wrinkled and folded to give a bigger surface for taking in oxygen and releasing carbon dioxide.

# SEA SNAKE

Sea snakes are so suited to life in water that most cannot move on land. They look more like eels than snakes, with flattened bodies and paddle-like tails for swimming. They live the whole of their lives in the sea, regularly coming to the surface to breathe. They have large lungs that are used for breathing, but also for buoyancy in the water.

Bluefin tuna

# HORSESHOE CRAB

With ancestors dating back around 450 million years, horseshoe crabs are among the oldest animals on Earth. They are not really crabs at all, but are closely related to spiders and scorpions. They live in coastal waters but, twice a year, large numbers of crabs come ashore to breed.

# ORCA
## ORCINUS ORCA

### HARBOR SEAL
To help them avoid hungry orcas, these seals can see and hear better underwater than they can on land!

With their sleek black-and-white bodies, orcas are striking creatures. Also known as killer whales, they are in fact the largest members of the dolphin family. This male orca lives in the Pacific Ocean, off the northwest coast of North America. It weighs around 10 tons and eats an impressive 485 pounds of food a day.

These intelligent, social creatures live in groups of up to 30, called pods, communicating with each other using clicks, whistles, and other calls. Orcas are fast, streamlined hunters that swim at a top speed of 30 mph. They prey on sea mammals—such as seals and sea lions—fish, sharks, squid, sea turtles, stingrays, and even large whales! Some orcas chase prey for long distances until it becomes exhausted. Others work together to round up fish, and then stun them by slapping their tails.

### GIANT SEA BASS
These gentle giants live near kelp and rocky reefs. They eat stingrays, sharks, and crabs, among other creatures.

### SEA OTTER
These mammals eat sea urchins, which stops them from eating too much of the kelp forest.

What an orca chooses to eat for dinner can have a huge effect on its habitat. If seals and sea lions are hard to find, orcas will eat sea otters instead. These furry mammals prey mainly on spiky sea urchins, and sea urchins eat kelp (a tall seaweed). If orcas eat too many sea otters, the urchins will flourish without their predators, eating and destroying whole underwater forests of kelp!

### BRITTLE STAR
Clinging to the seabed, brittle stars scavenge for tiny sea plants and animals.

Rock greenling

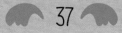

# AMERICAN ALLIGATOR
## ALLIGATOR MISSISSIPPIENSIS

Lurking in the marshy Everglades, an enormous swamp in Florida, this American alligator is one of the largest reptiles on Earth. It can grow up to 10 feet long, can weigh up to half a ton, and its tail is strong enough to knock a human off their feet!

This armor-plated reptile is well suited for aquatic life. Its olive-green coloring makes good camouflage in the swampy water, and its sturdy limbs and webbed toes are perfect for swimming. It lies half-submerged in the water waiting for prey—its eyes and snout are on the top of its head so that it can still see and breathe. With massive jaws and sharp teeth, the alligator is a fearsome predator that feasts on fish, frogs, snakes, and passing mammals, such as bobcats or raccoons.

Alligators have a huge effect on their environment. The swamps dry up for part of the year, so using its snout and tail, the alligator digs a large hole that fills up with water and stays full even when the rains stop. As well as offering the alligator protection from the hot weather, the water hole also provides a drink for thirsty turtles and snakes—and these creatures then supply the alligator with food.

When the weather changes and the alligator no longer needs its "gator hole," smaller animals move in, for shelter and to breed.

White ibis

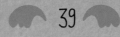

### GREAT BLUE HERON
Standing tall, these elegant birds wade through swamps, searching for fish to eat, including the blue catfish.

### BOBCAT
Solitary bobcats prey stealthily on raccoons at night and create dens in caves or hollow trees.

### RACCOON
Raccoons eat plants and small animals. They often catch food in water and can swim if they need to.

### BLUE CATFISH
This is the largest of the catfish species, and it often hunts for wounded fish at nighttime.

# SOUTHERN ELEPHANT SEAL
## *MIROUNGA LEONINA*

Southern elephant seals spend most of their lives at sea. They regularly dive to depths of around 1,640 feet, and can hold their breath for more than an hour while they hunt. Male and female southern elephant seals hunt in different places. Males hunt on the sea floor, while females go fishing in the middle region of the sea. They eat mostly fish and squid, but populations of king crab have moved to the Antarctic, providing the seals with another source of food.

Male elephant seals are the biggest seals in the world, weighing more than 4 tons. They are named after their enormous noses, which remind people of elephant's trunks. At breeding time, males inflate their noses and make a loud bellowing sound to warn off rivals.

In spring, enormous groups of these seals gather on the rocky beaches of South Georgia, a remote island in the southern Atlantic Ocean. They haul themselves out of the water to breed and raise their young. They can often be seen surrounded by colonies of king penguins. The impressive, stately wandering albatross also visits this remote island to breed every other year. When the seal pups reach one month old, their mothers head back to the ocean. The seal pups follow a few weeks later, watching out for hungry leopard seals as they head into the sea.

King penguins

### WANDERING ALBATROSS
These huge birds spend most of their life in the air and have no predators!

### MACARONI PENGUINS
With a diet of crabs, fish, and seals, these penguins compete with elephant seals for certain foods.

### LEOPARD SEAL
These fierce hunters sometimes prey on baby southern elephant seals.

### SQUID
Squid live deep in the ocean, so seals have adapted brilliant diving skills to catch them.

# EURASIAN OTTER
## *LUTRA LUTRA*

The first sign of an otter in the water may be the long trail of bubbles it makes while slowly breathing out. This otter lives on the west coast of Scotland. Otters that live on the coast are usually active during the day when they hunt for food. Crabs, eels, and fish are their favorites but they will also eat water birds, like puffins.

Sleek and streamlined, with webbed feet and a powerful tail, the otter's body is perfectly adapted for swimming. Its fur is thick and waterproof to keep it warm, and it can close its eyes, ears, and nostrils to stop water getting in. These furry mammals spend most of their waking time in the water, which is where they find most of their food, but they can only hold their breath for a short time.

Eurasian otters can survive in lots of different habitats as long as there are fish for them to eat. If they spend a lot of time in saltwater, they will need to clean their fur in freshwater to make sure they stay waterproof.

Otters come ashore to sleep in holes they have burrowed, called holts. On land, otters leave five-toed footprints in the sand or mud. These excellent diggers also burrow tunnels underground, creating a safe route from their home to the nearest sea, river, lake, or swamp.

The otter competes with the harbor seal and even white-tailed eagles for food. The white-tailed eagle also eats fish and waterbirds, and has been known to swoop down and steal an otter's catch!

Eel

### HARBOR SEAL
When not preying on herring and cod, harbor seals can be found resting on the rocky shorelines.

### BASKING SHARK
These giant but harmless sharks often swim with their mouths wide open to catch plankton.

### ATLANTIC PUFFIN
Puffins are excellent swimmers and can dive underwater to catch sand eels and fish.

### ATLANTIC SALMON
Otters prey on these fish, which are known for migrating long distances.

# NARWHAL
## MONODON MONOCEROS

Narwhals are known as "unicorns of the sea" because hundreds of years ago, their long, spiraling tusks were mistaken for unicorn horns. These extraordinary creatures are in fact related to dolphins, belugas, and orcas.

The narwhal's sword-like tusk is an overgrown tooth. Not all females have them, but in males, these can grow to more than 6.5 feet long, right through the narwhal's upper lip. No one is sure what the tusks are used for. They may be for impressing females or for fighting off rival males—and they also provide homes for tiny sea plants!

Narwhals live year round in the icy waters of the Arctic Ocean around Canada, Greenland, and Russia. They travel in groups of up to 20 but can sometimes gather in their hundreds, or even thousands. The members of the group communicate with each other with clicks and whistles.

During winter, narwhals feed on flatfish underneath thick pack ice, but they have to keep moving to avoid getting trapped when the sea freezes over.

In summer, they eat mostly Arctic cod, polar cod, and halibut. They are fantastic divers and can swim for a mile beneath water before coming up for air. Their main enemies are orcas, but the polar bears and walruses that they share their habitat with sometimes hunt narwhals, too. The Greenland shark has been known to follow groups of narwhals to pick off the dead and dying members of the pod, but they do not usually attack them.

Polar cod

45

### WALRUS
Preferring the freezing cold, walruses chase the ice packs as they move around the Arctic Circle each year.

### GREENLAND SHARK
These enormous sharks can live for hundreds of years! They scavenge the ocean for dead and dying animals to eat.

### ARCTIC COD
Sometimes found under pack ice, this fish is a stable part of the narwhal's diet.

### GREENLAND TURBOT
Cold-water predators, such as the Greenland shark, hunt these deep-sea fish.

# GIANT CLAM
## TRIDACNA GIGAS

Sitting on the sandy floor of the Great Barrier Reef off the coast of Australia, this giant clam is an impressive sight. It is the largest mollusk in the world, weighing a whopping 440 pounds, and measuring more than 40 feet across. It will stay anchored to this spot for the rest of its life—which can be up to 100 years!

Its thick shell is made from two parts, held together by strong muscles. These muscles pull the shell shut if the clam senses danger. In between the two sides of the shell, the clam's mantle is colored yellow, green, or golden brown, where it is covered by billions of tiny plants that live there.

Nudibranch

These plants provide the clam with the nourishing food that helps it to reach its huge size. In return, the clam offers the plants a home safe from the animals that eat them, and in the daytime, opens up so that the plants can soak up sunlight to make their food. Lobsters and crabs living nearby also eat the food produced by these plants. Young reef fish also take shelter in the giant clam to protect themselves from larger predators.

Although they are stationary creatures, giant clams help to build the coral reefs around them. They make and give off large amounts of the material that shells and coral are made of, which help these nearby creatures to stay strong. Giant clams also catch and eat tiny animals that float past, filtering the water around them. They are essential for healthy coral reefs!

### REEF SHARK
By day, small fish use reef sharks as scratching posts! But by night, these sharks are determined hunters.

### CORAL TROUT
Tiny fish eat bacteria from a coral trout's skin, which keeps the trout clean and also feeds the fish.

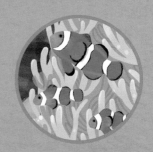

### CLOWN FISH
These small fish live safely within venomous anemones without being stung. This protects them from hunters.

### STINGRAY
Stingrays have mouths on the bottom side of their body to catch clams, shrimp, and mussels.

# EMPEROR PENGUIN
## APTENODYTES FORSTERI

Standing more than 3 feet tall, the Emperor penguin is the largest species of penguin. It lives on the pack ice and coasts of Antarctica, where it feeds on krill, fish, like the bald notothen and Antarctic silverfish, and glacial squid.

This majestic bird is clumsy when on land, but its streamlined body is brilliantly adapted for swimming, with flipper-like wings and a stiff tail for steering. To keep warm in its icy home, it has a thick layer of blubber under its skin, and its feathers are both windproof and waterproof.

Emperor penguins share their habitat with orcas and leopard seals, both of which sometimes prey on them. Penguins also have to watch out for south polar skuas. These coastal birds will swoop down and eat the eggs, and even the newborn chicks, of Emperor penguins.

These birds need to be incredibly hardy—they breed on the ice in the freezing mid-winter. Once a female has laid an egg, she goes off to sea to feed. The male then balances the egg on his feet, tucked under a warm flap of skin. For the next two months, thousands of males huddle together, taking turns to move to the warmer center of the huddle. When the chicks are due to hatch, the females return. Then the males head to sea for a welcome meal, and to bring back food for the chick, too.

Antarctic silverfish

**BALD NOTOTHEN**
The bald notothen forages for krill, just under the surface of the ice.

**SOUTH POLAR SKUA**
These birds sometimes prey on the eggs of Emperor penguins, as well as on krill.

**ANTARCTIC KRILL**
Krill are at the very bottom of the food chain. Without them, a lot of creatures would go hungry.

**GLACIAL SQUID**
Emperor penguins compete with seals, albatrosses, and other Antarctic predators to feed on squid.

# MARINE IGUANA
## *AMBLYRHYNCHUS CRISTATUS*

Sunbathing on a rock by the sea, this marine iguana from the Galápagos Islands is warming up, ready for a busy day searching for food. These islands provide reptiles with the perfect warm climate for their cold-blooded bodies, and iguanas can sometimes be seen laying out on coastal rocks in their hundreds.

Marine iguanas are the only lizards to feed in the sea. They have flattened tails for swimming and can hold their breath for more than half an hour. They dive into the water and scrape off algae from rocks with their blunt noses and small, sharp teeth, sharing this food source with the Galápaos green turtle. Some individuals grow larger than others depending on how much they eat. The more they eat, the more they grow! Back on land, the iguanas can be heard sneezing the sea salt from their noses in puffs. They accidentally eat salty seawater as they feed, and too much salt can be harmful for them.

At breeding time, the females lay their eggs inland, in deep burrows in the sand or volcanic ash. Baby marine iguanas are able to fend for themselves as soon as they have hatched, and have to guard against Galápagos lava gulls and Galápagos racer snakes. These sneaky creatures emerge from cracks in the rocks and chase after them. As they grow up, these iguanas also defend themselves against the Galápagos hawk.

Galápagos hawk

51

### GALÁPAGOS SEA LION
Sea lions are a very common sight on the Galápagos Islands. They hunt for fish near the shore.

### GALÁPAGOS RACER SNAKE
These speedy and slightly venomous snakes prey on lizards, iguanas, mice, and baby birds.

### GALÁPAGOS GREEN TURTLE
Preyed on by birds and sharks, newly hatched turtles have a tough start in life!

### GALÁPAGOS LAVA GULL
This rare bird only lives on the Galápagos Islands. It eats fish and preys on young marine iguanas.

# TRIPLEWART SEADEVIL
## CRYPTOPSARAS COUESII

The depths of the Atlantic Ocean are pitch black because sunlight is unable to reach that deep under water. But some deep-sea creatures can make their own light, like this female deep-sea anglerfish, the triplewart seadevil.

This luminous creature has a long fin, like a fishing rod, growing from its snout, which it moves back and forth. At the end is a glowing blob of light made up of millions of light-making bacteria. As well as showing the fish what's coming up ahead, the light also tempts prey toward the fish's open mouth, as they mistake the light for a tasty snack.

The female deep-sea anglerfish can grow up to one foot long. It has a huge mouth and an expandable stomach for eating prey much larger than itself. Food is tricky to find in this harsh environment, so this adaptation helps the fish stock up whenever prey is available. It mainly eats fish and squid, but will eat spiky crustaceans, too.

Its mouth is lined with rows of long, curved, see-through teeth that can point inward so that prey accidentally swims in. These teeth then spring back into place, like prison bars, to stop fish or squid escaping. Male anglerfish are much smaller than females, and they do not have the glowing fishing rods.

Other animals that live that far deep down in the ocean have also evolved to catch prey using special adaptations like light.

Flabby whalefish

### VIPERFISH
Viperfish light up the ocean, too. They have lights behind their eyes and along the sides of their bodies.

### COMMON FANGTOOTH
This menacing fish grabs and hangs onto any prey that passes it with its sharp teeth.

### PELICAN EEL
Using their glowing tails to lure prey, pelican eels dislocate their jaws to swallow creatures whole!

### AMPHIPOD
These shrimp-like crustaceans live deep in the ocean. They scavenge for animals that have just died.

# GREAT WHITE SHARK
## CARCHARODON CARCHARIAS

This great white shark lives off the coast of California and is built for hunting. It has a sleek, streamlined body and a powerful tail for swimming up to 25 mph. Its mouth is lined with hundreds of razor-sharp, serrated teeth, arranged in rows. While growing up, the great white shark will eat small fish and rays, but once it has reached full maturity, turtles, dolphins, larger fish, like the bluefin tuna, seals, sea lions, and small whales will also be on the menu.

It uses its extraordinary sense of smell to locate prey and can detect a weak or injured animal from many miles away. Once it has reached its prey, it attacks rapidly, shaking its head from side to side to saw off chunks of flesh. Though they are usually solitary, sharks can sometimes gather in groups around a carcass. Despite their reputation, great white sharks very rarely attack humans. Humans pose more of a danger to them!

Great white sharks live in cool, coastal waters all around the world. They grow to an average of 16 feet long. Fearsome predators such as these are important for the ocean ecosystem as they control the numbers of all of the animals they eat. Without sharks, the sea lions may eat all of their fish prey and could starve or be forced to move on to find food elsewhere.

California sea lion

**OCEAN SUNFISH**
This huge, heavy, round fish often relies on small fish and birds to snack on the parasites that cling to it.

**DUSKY DOLPHIN**
Often seen performing acrobatics, dusky dolphins hunt in packs. Sometimes sharks will steal their catch.

**ORCA**
Killer whales are at the top of their food chain and sometimes prey on great white sharks!

**BLUEFIN TUNA**
Great white sharks hunt bluefin tuna, but few other hunters can catch up with these fast fish.

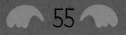

# ANIMALS IN THE AIR

Being able to fly or glide has allowed large numbers of animals—mostly birds and insects—to take to the air in their habitats, as they move about looking for food and escaping from enemies.

## BIRDS

All birds have wings and feathers, and most can fly, though not all. Their wing shapes and ways of flying have adapted to their habitats and lifestyles, the food they eat, and the predators they face.

## BATS

Bats are the only mammals that can truly fly by flapping their wings. Their wings are made from leathery skin, stretched across their finger and toe bones.

## INSECTS

Dragonflies are champion fliers of the insect world. They have two pairs of long, transparent wings which they hold out when they perch. They can beat each pair on their own, allowing them to hover, change direction in mid-air, and fly backwards.

## HUMMINGBIRDS

Hummingbirds get their name from the humming sound their wings make because they beat so quickly. To hover in mid-air, a hummingbird may beat its wings more than 80 times a second. These tiny birds hover in front of flowers, to feed on the sweet nectar inside.

## FLYING LEMURS

Flying lemurs, or colugos, live in the rainforest. They cannot truly fly but can glide long distances from tree to tree to find food. Broad folds of skin, attached to their long limbs and tail, spread out like a parachute. Gliding is useful in the rainforest where the trees are often tall and widely spaced.

## PUFFINS

Puffins are stocky birds, which live, breed, and feed along the coast. They have short wings that they have to beat quickly for flying low over the surface of the sea, looking for fish to catch. They also use their wings for swimming underwater.

# BARN OWL
## TYTO ALBA

An expert hunter, this barn owl is on the lookout for its next meal. It mostly feeds on small rodents, such as field mice and shrews, but will also catch rabbits, moles, and even fish and smaller birds. Barn owls are perfectly adapted to hunting at night, with hearing so sensitive that they can stalk prey in the pitch dark, using sound alone. To catch their prey, they will fly slowly and silently, then swoop down to the ground, grabbing their prey in their sharp talons.

Though they sometimes hunt during the day, this can be tricky as other birds, such as magpies, are known to "mob" them if they see them out during the day—flying around them in groups to stop them hunting.

Barn owls are sometimes hunted themselves by larger birds of prey—even by other owls, such as the eagle owl. They also have to protect their eggs from predators, such as snakes and stoats, who sneak into their nests for a meal while the parents are out hunting.

Barn owls usually nest in pairs. A female barn owl will lay her eggs in a hollow tree or a farm building, to keep them safe and warm. She feeds the chicks with food brought by the male and stays with them until they have grown the soft, downy feathers that will keep them warm. She also teaches them how to hunt and find food for themselves.

Shrew, vole, and field mouse

**MAGPIE**

These clever birds adapt to almost any environment, hunting smaller birds and even eating from bins!

**COMMON BUZZARD**

Buzzards will hunt almost anything, from rabbits and pheasants to snakes and lizards.

**SHORT-TAILED VOLE**

Barn owls, kestrels, buzzards, and stoats all feed on these tiny rodents.

**EAGLE OWL**

The eagle owl is one of the biggest owls in the world and can be extremely territorial.

# ARCTIC TERN
## STERNA PARADISAEA

With its black cap, red beak, and white body, the Arctic tern has striking looks, but this is not its only claim to fame. Each year, this globe-trotter makes the longest migration of any bird, flying from the Arctic to Antarctica and back again. Between its two flights, it spends eight months of every year in the air, covering a staggering 25,000 miles. In its lifetime, an Arctic tern will fly the same incredible distance as three trips to the Moon and back.

Arctic terns breed around the Arctic Ocean, during the arctic summer. To impress a female, male terns will perform amazing feats of acrobatics in the air, then present her with a fish. She lays her eggs on a patch of grass, which both parents fiercely defend from predators, such as Arctic foxes and herring gulls. The Arctic tern has to compete with herring gulls, northern gannets, and other larger birds for nesting sites on beaches, rocks, and in forests, and for the fish and crustaceans they eat.

As winter comes, the terns fly south to Antarctica to spend another summer there (while it is winter in the Arctic, it is summer in Antarctica). There, they feed on the plentiful supplies of fish in the Southern Ocean before it is time to head north again. As there is no native plant life in Antarctica, and therefore not many animals, there is far less competition for food from other birds.

Arctic tern and chicks

### HERRING GULL
These opportunistic eaters steal food from Arctic terns and other birds.

### ARCTIC FOX
Arctic foxes will hunt almost everything, from birds and fish to baby seals.

### NORTHERN GANNET
These birds dive into the ocean for food, and tiny airbags under their skin help them return to the surface.

### LITTLE AUK
One of the many birds competing for fish and crustaceans in the Arctic, this little bird hunts in large colonies.

# FLYING LEMUR
## CYNOCEPHALUS VOLANS

At night, in the Philippine rain forest, a secretive creature takes to the air. It is called a flying lemur—but it isn't a lemur, and doesn't truly fly. The Philippine flying lemur, also known as the colugo, is an extraordinary mammal that glides between the trees to find food. A huge, wing-like flap of skin reaches from its neck to the tips of its fingers and toes, and down to the tip of its tail. As the flying lemur launches itself from a branch, this skin stretches out in the shape of a kite.

By day, the flying lemur rests in a tree hole or clings onto a branch high up in the tree canopy with its strong, sharp claws. At dusk, it climbs up the tree trunk and glides off in search of leaves, berries, and flowers to eat. The flying lemur is a herbivore, feeding on the abundant fruits and flowers of the Philippine rain forest. Though the rain forest is full of food, the flying lemur must compete with hundreds of other plant-eating animals, such as tree shrews and fruit bats, for it.

Its huge eyes have adapted to help it see in the dark. It must keep a lookout for its main predator, the Philippine eagle, as well as eagle owls and tree-climbing snakes that will try to catch it as it leaps from tree to tree.

Eagle owl

 63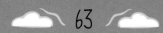

### TREE SHREW
They may look similar to mice or voles, but these little herbivores are actually primates, like monkeys.

### PHILIPPINE TARSIER
This small mammal feeds on insects, which in turn protects the plants eaten by other rainforest creatures.

### PHILIPPINE EAGLE
Philippine eagles hunt monkeys and flying lemurs as they search for fruit and leaves to eat.

### GOLDEN CROWNED FRUIT BAT
These bats eat figs and other fruits, then fly across the rainforest, helping these fruits to spread their seeds.

# ALBATROSS
## DIOMEDEA SANFORDI

Soaring high above the Southern Ocean, this northern royal albatross is one of the world's biggest flying birds, with a whopping wingspan of more than 10 feet. Its glides above the water, on the lookout for food. It mostly eats squid and fish, which it snatches from the surface of the sea with its strong, hooked bill. There is a lot of competition for food from sea lions and other fish-eating animals (like whales or penguins), so often albatrosses feed on by-catch, discarded by fishing boats. In fact, they are known to follow boats in the hope of finding food.

Northern royal albatrosses are long-lived birds and can reach the age of 60 years old in the wild. These albatrosses usually pair up for life, winning over a mate with an impressive flying display. They only nest in New Zealand, returning to the same site year after year where they form large colonies. They build their nests from mud, plants, and feathers, and lay a single egg inside. The chick hatches after about 80 days and is ready to leave the nest after eight months. Living in a colony is important to the birds' survival, allowing them to share the work of incubating the eggs and rearing the chicks while others go out to sea to find food.

Staying in big groups also helps to keep the albatross safe. Very few animals hunt these enormous birds, but tiger sharks have been known to snatch up young albatrosses learning to fly over the sea.

Stoat

### LITTLE BLUE PENGUIN
Little penguins are home to a species of mite, which live in their feathers and feed on the special oil there.

### HUMPBACK WHALE
These whales are harmless gentle giants—unless you're a tiny fish!

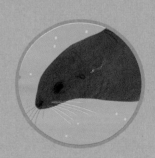

### HOOKER'S SEA LION
These sea lions can adapt to their environment and will eat whatever's available.

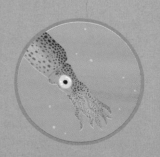

### SQUID
Squid is an important food source for albatrosses, little blue penguins, and many other marine creatures.

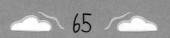

# HYACINTH MACAW
## *ANODORHYNCHUS HYACINTHINUS*

This hyacinth macaw lives in the Pantanal, a huge swamp in southwest Brazil. It feeds on nuts from the local palm trees, which it crushes with its very strong, sharp beak. Hyacinth macaws are large parrots, growing around 3 feet long from the tops of their heads to the tips of their long tails. They are beautiful birds, with bright blue feathers and yellow markings around their eyes and beak.

At breeding time, the macaws make their nests inside holes in hollow trees. There is fierce competition for the best nesting sites from toco toucans and other birds. The nest is filled with soft sawdust, and the female lays one or two eggs, though, usually, only one chick survives. Hyacinth macaw eggs are eaten by many predators, such as coatis, opossums, capuchin monkeys, and, occasionally, green iguanas. If they survive, the chicks leave their nests at around three months old, once they have learned to fly and find food for themselves.

Today, the hyacinth macaw is in serious danger in the wild. Though no other animals hunt it for food, it is at risk from one major predator—humans. Its habitat is being cleared to make space for farms and living space. Large numbers of macaws are also caught illegally and sold as pets. The hyacinth macaw is now protected by law in Brazil.

Toco toucan

**MARSH DEER**
These deer travel around, uncovering different foods by the water.

**TUFTED CAPUCHIN**
Capuchins aren't picky— they'll eat eggs, nuts, lizards, and even bats!

**GIANT OTTER**
Giant otters are apex predators, hunting crabs, snakes, caimans, and even huge anacondas.

**YACARE CAIMAN**
Related to crocodiles, caimans lurk in the river, ambushing prey, but risk attack from anacondas and jaguars.

# PIPISTRELLE BAT
## *PIPISTRELLUS PIPISTRELLUS*

At dusk, tiny pipistrelle bats flit quickly yet jerkily through the air on the hunt for food. These bats feed on small moths, lacewings, and other insects, which they find by giving out a series of high-pitched clicks, then listening out for the echoes as the sound hits objects in its path. This is called echolocation.

Pipistrelles live in gardens, woodlands, and over water, where insect life is rife, in Britain and other parts of Europe. During the day, they roost in oak, ash, and beech trees and under the eaves of buildings. They are active from March to November. In winter, when food is scarce, they hibernate in cracks in buildings and trees, as well as specially-made bat boxes in people's gardens. Here, they are safe from the cold and rain, and from weasels and other predators.

Young bats are born in June and July. They feed on their mothers' milk for 3-4 weeks, and are able to fly when they are about four weeks old.

A single pipstrelle can eat 3,000 insects in a single night! This plays a vital part in keeping its environment running smoothly, as it helps keep the insect population down. Without this tiny bat, the woodlands would be overrun with insects, which would eat all available foliage, leaving no food for plant-eating animals such as Muntjac deer.

Weasel

### JAY
These birds store acorns and other food in caches to save them for later.

### TAWNY OWL
If you see a tawny owl, chances are there are no smaller owls in the area, as tawnies will scare them off!

### MUNTJAC DEER
Deer munching on the branches and roots of trees and bushes encourages them to grow.

### BADGER
Badgers can break into wasp nests and bee hives for a snack, their fur protecting them from stings.

# GILA WOODPECKER
## MELANERPES UROPYGIALIS

The Sonoran Desert in the southwestern United States is home to the magnificent gila woodpecker. This striking-looking bird has a brown face and chest, a black-and-white striped back, and the male has a bright red cap of feathers.

Gila woodpeckers mainly eat insects, which they catch with their long, pointed beaks and sticky tongues, but will also feed on cactus fruits and berries. Woodpeckers that venture near people's houses have even been known to steal dog food. In turn, gila woodpeckers are a major food source for many desert predators, including bobcats, coyotes, and large, carnivorous lizards called gila monsters.

Gila woodpeckers shelter from the hot desert sun in giant saguaro cacti, in holes that they dig out with their beaks. Like all woodpeckers, their heads and neck muscles are very strong to allow them to break through the tough cactus. Inside the cactus, where it is cooler, they lay 3–5 eggs in April or May. The woodpeckers cannot move in immediately—the hole needs to dry out first—so they must start digging the hole before they are ready to lay their eggs.

Once a woodpecker has left the cactus, the holes quite often provide a home for great horned owls, flycatchers, and other birds.

Prickly pear

### ROADRUNNER
These birds are one of the only animals quick enough to catch rattlesnakes.

### MEXICAN GRAY WOLF
Gray wolves are very rare in the Sonoran Desert due to hunting by humans.

### GILA MONSTER
These carnivorous lizards don't need to eat very often—they can store fat in their tails.

### TIGER RATTLESNAKE
Tiger rattlesnakes kill lizards and rodents by biting them and injecting them with deadly venom.

# RAGGIANA BIRD-OF-PARADISE

### *PARADISAEA RAGGIANA*

Deep in the rain forests of Papua New Guinea lives a group of birds with such magnificent feathers that they were once believed to come from paradise! Among them is the Raggiana bird-of-paradise. It is the national bird of Papua New Guinea and is seen as so important that it even appears on the country's flag.

Raggiana birds-of-paradise live high up in the trees, feeding on the rich supplies of fruit, insects, and spiders. It helps to carry the seeds of the fruit it eats across the rain forest (in the birds' droppings), allowing new plants to grow. This, in turn, provides food and shelter for thousands of other birds and animals.

At breeding time, they really put on a show. Males are famous for their spectacular feathers that they display to compete with other males and win over a female. As the females look on, the males hang upside-down from the branches, clapping their wings and fanning out their fabulous tails. Other birds-of-paradise have similar methods. The superb bird-of-paradise raises its tail feathers in a way that makes it look like a strange smiley face and then dances around the female.

Female birds-of-paradise are much less colorful than males. This helps to camouflage them among the trees when they sit on their nests.

Female superb bird-of-paradise

### QUEEN ALEXANDRA BIRDWING BUTTERFLY
These butterflies only live for a few months.

### TREE KANGAROO
Tree kangaroos are slow and clumsy on the ground but can clamber up trees quickly and nimbly.

### BOWERBIRD
Male bowerbirds decorate their nests with brightly colored objects to impress a female.

### LONG-BEAKED ECHIDNA
These strange mammals mostly feed on insects and earthworms on the forest floor.

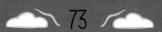

# LESSER FLAMINGO
## PHOENICOPARRUS MINOR

Flamingos are easy to recognize, with their pink feathers and long legs and neck. They are wading birds that live around salty lakes or coasts. They feed on shrimp and also on tiny plants called algae, which give them their distinctive pink color. To find food, a flamingo uses its feet to stir up the mud. It then puts its head down, so that its beak is upside down in the water, and sweeps it from side to side. Using its tongue, it pumps water in and out of its beak, sieving out tiny items of food.

Flamingos are very sociable birds, and live in huge flocks. Hundreds of thousands of lesser flamingos like these gather on the shores of Lake Natron in Tanzania, Africa, to breed. They lay their eggs in cone-shaped nests of mud to protect the eggs from being washed away by flooding. After the chicks hatch, they collect in groups and are looked after by an adult while the others find food.

Staying in big numbers helps to protect flamingos from the many predators that hunt them. Flamingos are preyed on by spotted hyenas, maribou storks, African golden wolves, African fish eagles, and many other predators.

Baby lesser flamingo

### MARIBOU STORK
Adult flamingos and chicks are caught and eaten by massive maribou storks.

### AFRICAN FISH EAGLE
African fish eagles mainly eat fish but will also prey on lesser flamingos.

### SPOTTED HYENA
Spotted hyenas are skilled hunters that chase down flamingos until they are exhausted, then eat them.

### WHITE LIPPED TILAPIA
The white-lipped tilapia is one of very few fish that can survive in salty Lake Natron.

# CONDOR
## VULTUR GRYPHUS

This Andean condor is a massive bird, with huge, black wings spanning more than 10 feet. Too heavy to fly without help, it lives in the windy Andes mountains in South America, where it can glide on warm air currents to keep it aloft. It roosts on a cliff face during the night, then spends most of the day soaring high above the peaks, only needing to flap its wings once every hour or so.

Andean condors have glossy black feathers, with a white collar around their neck and a bald head. They have extremely sharp eyesight for spotting food from high up in the air. They will look out for clues, such as vultures or other birds of prey circling in the sky. Condors mainly eat carrion of large animals, such as llamas, deer, and armadillos, tearing carcasses apart with their strong claws and sharp, hooked beak, and picking the bones clean. After eating, they rub their heads and necks across the ground to get them clean. Often, they eat the remains of other predators' food.

Though Andean condors have no natural predators in the wild, their eggs are often eaten by foxes. They are also in danger from humans, as they are hunted and killed by farmers trying to protect their livestock.

Armadillo

### YELLOW-HEADED VULTURE
Like condors, vultures are scavengers that feed on the leftovers of dead animals.

### LLAMA
Llamas form bonds with other animals and will protect them from attackers.

### BLACK VULTURE
Black vultures will group up to steal carcasses from other vultures like the turkey vulture.

### MARMOTS
These herbivores can store extra fat in their bellies for winter when food is scarce.

# GLOSSARY

## Adaptation

The way a living thing changes to survive and thrive in its environment

## Aloft

In the air or sky

## Armor

A protective covering used to prevent damage or harm

## Barren

Land unable to produce much or any vegetation

## Buoyancy

The ability to float in water

## Bycatch

Fish or other creatures unintentionally caught while fishing for other species

## Camouflage

Blending in with the surrounding environment

## Carcass

The dead body of an animal

## Carnivorous

An animal that eats meat; a carnivore

## Carrion

The decaying flesh of a dead animal

## Climate

The most frequent weather conditions of a specific place

## Cold-blooded

An animal whose body temperature changes with the environment

## Communicate

Share and exchange information, either verbally or through body language

## Crustaceans

A type of arthopod, like crabs, lobsters, crayfish, shrimp, krill, and more

## Display

Part of the mating courtship in which an animal tries to attract a mate. This can include showing off their beauty or strength and special movements or vocalizations

## Ecosystem

A community of animals that interact with each other and their environment

## Environment

The area in which a plant, animal, or person lives

## Excreting

A way of getting rid of waste from the body

## Evolution

The gradual changes in a species caused by different circumstances in its life and environment

## Habitat

The home of an animal, plant, or person

## Hibernating

Spending the winter in a dormant state, asleep, until it is warm enough or until there is enough food to come out again

## Hierarchy

The ranking of members of a group by authority, age, or other status

## Holts

An otter's den, sometimes called a couch

## Hostile

A feeling or environment that is uncomfortable or unsuitable

## Insectivorous

An animal that feeds on invertebrartes like insects or worms

## Migration

The seasonal movement of animals or insects from one place to another

## Nourishing

Eating food that is necessary to grow and live healthily

## Poaching

Illegally hunting or trapping wild animals

## Predator

An animal that preys on another

## Prey

An animal that is hunted and killed for food

## Resources

A supply of food, water, and shelter—everything needed for an animal to stay alive

## Roost

Where a bird or bat rests at night—usually on a nest or in a tree

## Solitary

The only one

## Streamlined

A body shape that gives little or no resistance to air or water, allowing for more speed and movement

## Submerged

To be underwater

## Tusk

A long, pointed tooth on the outside of the mouth, usually found on animals like elephants

## Tundra

A large, barren piece of land with no trees or vegetation

## Wounded

To have been injured

## Venomous

An animal that is able to inject venom into another by biting or stinging it

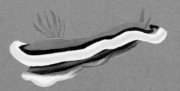

# CREDITS

## WRITTEN BY ANITA GANERI

Anita Ganeri has written over 300 books for children. She lives in York, England with her husband, son, daughter, three dogs, and a cat.

## ILLUSTRATED BY MADDY VIAN

Maddy Vian is an independent artist that spends her days creating colorful illustrations from her seaside home near Margate, England. She graduated from Kingston School of Art with a degree in Illustration Animation and has continued to have a prolific start to her career. *Animal Worlds of Wonder* is her first published picture book. She likes her work to celebrate positivity and use every color under the sun.